BRONNER'S
CHRISTmas Wonderland

Ornament Legends Symbols & Traditions

The Bronner team researched and edited the legends, symbols, and traditions for this book with the hope that they will bring special meaning to your Christmas decorating. First published in 2004, this updated edition includes 28 new entries for a total of 100. Ornaments representing each of these unique themes can be found at Bronner's CHRISTmas Wonderland, the world's largest Christmas store, located in Frankenmuth, Michigan.

Visit the website at www.bronners.com for more information about Bronner's.

Research and Editing:
BRONNER'S CHRISTmas WONDERLAND

Illustrations* by
Connie V. Larsen

*with the exception of "our Lady of Czestochowa" and "Our Lady of Guadalupe" which are representations of the actual religious icons.

Symbol of the
Acorn

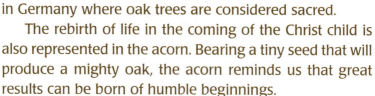

The acorn has long been considered a symbol of good luck in Germany where oak trees are considered sacred.

The rebirth of life in the coming of the Christ child is also represented in the acorn. Bearing a tiny seed that will produce a mighty oak, the acorn reminds us that great results can be born of humble beginnings.

Legend of the
Apple

The apple played an important role in traditional European Christmas Eve celebrations. Following dinner, the head of the family would slice an apple crosswise. If the slice revealed the image of a perfect star and the seeds were plump, it was believed that a peaceful year of good fortune and health awaited the family. Each member of the family then ate a piece of the apple.

Tradition of the Bagpipes

Bagpipes are among the oldest musical instruments. Hundreds of types of bagpipes exist, each with a unique design and sound.

Associated with Scotland, bagpipes play a traditional role in modern Gaelic culture and are often played at military funerals and memorials. Weddings, parties and other social events are lifted by the sound of this unique musical instrument.

Symbol of the BEE

The bee is a symbol of industry, resourcefulness and prosperity.

These tiny creatures demonstrate the success and satisfaction found in working together harmoniously to enjoy the sweetness of life.

British farmers believed the bees hummed in honor of the Christ child on the first Christmas.

Tradition of Beer

Originating in ancient Egypt, beer is almost as old as civilization itself. In medieval times, monks brewed beer for a nourishing drink, which was permitted while fasting. Considered a valuable source of nutrition, beer played such an important role in daily lives that workers were often paid with jugs of beer. The brewing of beer is considered by many to be the oldest manufacturing art practiced by man.

Legend of Bigfoot

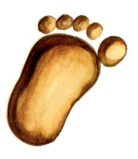

For hundreds of years, the legend of Bigfoot has been a subject of intrigue, with many sightings reported in remote areas worldwide. The tall half-man/half-ape is known as Bigfoot in the United States, Sasquatch (hairy giant) in Canada, and Yeti or Abominable Snowman in the Himalayas. Covered in long fur, Bigfoot received his name from reported discoveries of huge, human-like footprints up to 18 inches long.

Symbol of the
Bird Nest

A bird nest is a symbol of the home. It reminds us that we strive to make our home a place where family members grow and prosper. Considered a good luck symbol, the bird nest represents all the love and warmth, enthusiasm and commitment required in creating the happiest of homes.

Symbol of the
Bluebird

Throughout the world and throughout the ages, the bluebird has been viewed as a beautiful symbol of happiness, cheerfulness and joy. Considered a messenger of love and a harbinger of wonderful things to come, the bluebird seems to be attached to a wealth of uplifting sentiments. This small, delicate bird is a welcome sight, heralding prosperity, good fortune, good health, new birth and springtime's renewal.

Symbol of the Buffalo

To the American Indians, the buffalo symbolized the universe. Much of Indian life centered on the buffalo herd. Buffalo provided food, clothing, utensils and tools necessary in daily life. The Indians believed that a child whose name included the word "buffalo" would mature quickly, exhibit the strength of the buffalo, and become an extraordinary hunter.

Symbol of the Butterfly

Symbolic of resurrection and eternal life, the butterfly emerging from its cocoon represents the resurrection of Christ from the tomb. Just as the butterfly comes forth with a new body, those who trust in Christ come forth with new life.

The butterfly also represents flight, freedom and creative thinking. A symbol of spring, the butterfly truly reflects the beauty of nature.

Tradition of the
Candle

Before electric Christmas lights were invented, candles adorned the Christmas tree, sparkling like starlight against the dark green boughs.

The candle reminds us that Christ is the light of the world, bringing us out of the darkness of sin. Many European families still decorate their Christmas tree with candles that are burned on Christmas Eve.

Symbol of the
Candy Cane

The candy cane begins with a stick of white candy. The white symbolizes the purity of the Christmas season. Red stripes are for the blood shed by Christ on the cross so that we may have eternal life. The candy is formed into a "J" to represent the precious name of Jesus. It can also represent the staff of the Good Shepherd. Its hard consistency represents the Solid Rock, the foundation of the church, and the firmness of the promises of God.

Symbol of the
Cardinal

Christened the Christmas bird for its spectacular red color, the cardinal has become a symbol of the beauty and warmth of the holiday season. A glimpse of this brilliant bird brings cheer, hope and inspiration on a gray wintry day. As nature's reminder for us to focus on our faith, the cardinal's scarlet plumage represents the blood of Christ shed for the redemption of mankind.

Symbol of the
Carrot

The carrot, perhaps because of its association with the rabbit, symbolizes fertility and is believed to bring a bride good luck. Because of its rich nutritional value, the carrot also signifies nourishment. Its bright color characterizes the quality of standing out or being unique. Harvested from the earth as a root vegetable, the carrot suggests that seeking fulfillment may require a bit of digging or returning to our roots along life's way.

Legend of the
Cat

An old legend tells how a cat came with other wild animals to pay homage to the baby Jesus. Overcome by the glory of the Lord, the cat produced a trembling sound from its throat. One by one, the other creatures fled back to the wild, but the cat could not bring itself to leave. Since then, the cat has been a household companion, never forgetting its wild nature, but content in the comforts of a warm house.

Legend of the
Celtic
Cross

Most common in Ireland, Wales and Scotland, the Celtic cross is a symbol of both faith and ethnic heritage. The circle symbolizes eternity and God's endless love for man. Legend says that while preaching to the lost, St. Patrick was shown a sacred stone marked with a circle that was symbolic of the moon goddess. He drew a Latin cross within the circle and blessed the stone, making the first Celtic cross.

Tradition of the Chili Pepper

The chili pepper is a southwestern American tradition symbolizing warmth and friendship. Clusters of vibrantly colored chili peppers, called chili ristras, add a zesty flair to home décor. When hung near the door, chili peppers ensure a bountiful harvest; when placed in the kitchen, they bring good luck in cooking. Chilies are a spicy addition to many cuisines worldwide.

Legend of the Chimney Sweep

The hearth was always considered the center of the home. Since a chimney sweep not only cleaned the chimney, but also removed any harmful spirits, it was considered good luck for a bride to be kissed by a chimney sweep. It is also considered good luck for anyone to be touched by a chimney sweep, especially if he leaves you with a black smudge of soot!

Tradition of the
Chocolate Chip Cookie

The chocolate chip cookie was inadvertently created in 1930 by Ruth Graves Wakefield at the Toll House Inn in Whitman, MA. Lacking baking chocolate for her cookie recipe, she substituted a chopped semi-sweet chocolate bar, expecting it to melt into the batter during baking. The chocolate did not melt, and the cookie became an instant American classic. Ruth received a lifetime supply of chocolate for the rights to publish the recipe.

Legend of the
Christmas Bells

According to early legend, bells rang throughout the world announcing the birth of Christ. The ringing of bells during the joyous holiday season still adds delightful accompaniment to favorite carols and is a significant part of the Christmas celebration. High in their towers, suspended between heaven and earth, church bells have called the faithful to worship for centuries.

Legend of the
Christmas Rose

Rose ornaments on a Christmas tree are symbolic of beauty and are believed to be an expression of affection and love.

Legend tells us that a lowly shepherdess knelt at the manger, weeping because she had no gift to offer the newborn king. As her tears fell to earth, a rosebush sprang into bloom. She picked a bouquet of roses and offered them to the baby Jesus as her gift of love.

Legend of the
Christmas Spider

An old European Christmas legend tells of a poor woman unable to provide the traditional decorations for the special holiday. A spider made his home in her tree and began to spin beautiful webs. On Christmas morning, the first light of sun struck the cobwebs, turning them to silver. When the woman awoke, she found the tree was covered with silver treasure. The spider had brought good fortune!

Legend of the
Christmas Stocking

According to legend, a father was unable to provide his three daughters with a dowry. Hearing of their misfortune and wishing to help, St. Nicholas dropped three bags of gold coins down the chimney. The coins fell into each of the daughters' stockings, which were hanging by the fire to dry, providing a sufficient dowry. Since then, stockings hung by the fireplace are a traditional part of Christmas gift giving.

Symbol of the
Christmas Tree

Because it stays green all through the year, the evergreen tree is symbolic of the eternal life offered to Christians through faith in Christ. The treetop points heavenward. A star signifies the special star that guided the wise men to Bethlehem. Lights represent Christ, the light of the world. Gifts beneath the tree are representative of God's gift of his only begotten Son, who brings hope, love, joy and peace.

Symbol of the
Claddagh Ring

Originating in the Irish fishing village of Claddagh in the 17th century, the Claddagh ring is now used internationally as a token of friendship and love. The hand represents friendship and togetherness, the crown stands for loyalty, and the heart symbolizes love. Because of its history, unique design, and significant meanings, the Claddagh ring is often given and worn to celebrate many special occasions.

Symbol of the
Cow

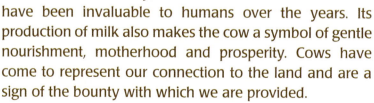

Regarded in some cultures as a symbol of status and bartered as currency, cows have been invaluable to humans over the years. Its production of milk also makes the cow a symbol of gentle nourishment, motherhood and prosperity. Cows have come to represent our connection to the land and are a sign of the bounty with which we are provided.

Tradition of the
Cowboy Boot

After the Civil War, the Western plains became home to massive cattle drives. Cowboys needed a boot that was designed for long hours on horseback. Boot makers created a boot with a pointed toe to easily slide into the stirrup, a slanted heel that hooks the stirrup, and a high top for protection. Still popular today, the cowboy boot has come to symbolize the free spirit of the American West.

Symbol of the
Cross

To Christians the cross symbolizes faith and salvation. Christians were granted the gift of eternal life in heaven when Jesus Christ was crucified on the cross for the sins of mankind and arose from the dead. Because Christ suffered pain and death on the cross, this divine and humbling symbol helps us to be mindful of our beliefs and duties as Christians. Faith in Christ helps us cope with the burden of the crosses we bear.

Tradition of the
Cuckoo Clock

Anton Ketterer designed and built the first cuckoo clock in the village of Schönwald, Germany, in the Black Forest around 1730. Ketterer reproduced the cuckoo bird's song with tiny twin goatskin bellows that blew into two tiny flutes. Hand carved during the winter, the clocks were popularized in the summer by peddlers who carried the clocks across Europe on their backs.

Our Lady of
Czestochowa

Legend says that St. Luke painted the portrait of Mary and Jesus known as "Our Lady of Czestochowa." It was brought to Poland in 1382 and kept at the shrine of Jasna Gora. In 1430 an attack on the shrine left the image with several gashes to the Madonna's face. Despite repeated attempts to repair them, they have always reappeared. Since that time there have been many miracles attributed to the painting. In 1656 King Jan Kazimierz proclaimed the shrine to be a spiritual capital for Poland. Through Poland's often painful history, it has been a symbol of hope in times of hardship. Today the shrine of Jasna Gora in Czestochowa continues to attract millions of visitors annually who honor its miraculous image.

Legend of the
Dogwood

At the time of Christ's crucifixion, the dogwood tree was a large, strong tree. Chosen to serve as the cross, the tree was greatly distressed. Sensing this, Jesus determined that the dogwood tree would never again grow large enough to become a cross. The dogwood tree blooms in the spring, often at Easter. Its blossom forms a cross and suggests the appearance of stained nail prints on the edge of each petal and a crown of thorns in the center of each flower.

Symbol of the
Dolphin

Because of their intelligence and playful ways, dolphins are one of Mother Nature's most fascinating creatures. Roman, Greek and Celtic cultures tell tales of dolphins' amazing ability to communicate with each other and even rescue drowning humans. Because they are friendly to man, dolphins represent the peace, harmony and tranquility that can be achieved in life.

Legend of the Donkey's Cross

Legend tells us that the donkey that carried Jesus into Jerusalem on Palm Sunday followed him to Calvary. Appalled by the sight of Jesus on the cross, the donkey turned away but could not leave. It is said that the shadow of the cross fell upon the shoulders and back of the donkey. A cross marking found on many donkeys today remains a testimony of the love and devotion of a humble, little donkey.

Symbol of the Dove

A universal symbol of peace and love, the dove has long held significance for man. Noah sent forth from the ark a dove that returned with an olive branch, indicating the end of the Flood and the beginning of God's covenant with man. The dove also symbolizes the Holy Spirit and signifies marriage and lifelong love. The pristine whiteness of the dove represents purity, hope for peace and the forgiveness we obtain from God and each other.

Symbol of the Dragonfly

The colors of the dragonfly sparkle with iridescence in the sunlight. Their jewel-like tones take time to develop, reflecting the idea that our own true colors only come forth with maturity. The dragonfly is found worldwide and in some cultures symbolizes new light and joy. Dragonflies are viewed as a representation of positive forces, renewal and the power of life.

Legend of the Dream Catcher

According to legend, Native Americans wove dream catchers and hung them above their sleeping places. Inspired by a spider weaving its web, dream catchers were believed to offer protection from bad dreams. Bad dreams became entangled in the web and disappeared with the first rays of the morning sun. Good dreams passed through the center of the dream catcher and were guided down to the sleeping person below.

Legend of the
Drummer Boy

Come, they told him to see the newborn king. The little drummer boy had no gift to bring so he played his drum – rum pum pum pum – for the holy child. The child smiled at the simple gift, reminding us that the best gifts come from the heart.

Symbol of the
Eagle

Immortalized in the sky as the constellation Aquilla, this heavenly eagle faces east towards the sun, showing us courage for meeting each new day. A majestic symbol, the eagle represents power, honor, strength and wisdom. The eagle became a national emblem in 1782 when the Great Seal of the United States was adopted. The eagle has come to represent freedom and bravery to Americans everywhere.

Legend of the
Edelweiss

According to Alpine folklore, suitors proved their love by climbing high crags of the Alps in search of the flower. Tragically, many suitors fell to their death or died of exposure to the weather. The edelweiss is still worn today as a symbol of love, bravery, strength and dedication. Because of its popularity with German and Austrian emperors, edelweiss is called the flower of emperors and kings.

Symbol of the
Elephant

The familiar phrase "An elephant never forgets" refers to the animal's alleged intelligence, memory and longevity. The peaceful elephant is also a symbol of gentle, reposing strength. The social nature of elephants allows us to view their amazing sensitivity to their group and family members, helping each other when hurt and mourning the loss of their loved ones.

Symbol of the Guardian Angel
Feather

The guardian angel feather symbolizes God's care for his people through the presence of angels. It is written in Psalm 91:11…"For he shall give his angels charge over thee, to keep thee in all thy ways."

Symbol of the
Fish

IXΘΥΣ

The letters of the Greek word for fish, "Ichthus," are the first letters of the Greek phrase for "Jesus Christ, God's Son, Savior." Accordingly, people use a fish symbol to distinguish themselves as Christians. Fish represent fertility and renewal of life. Just as fish are born in water, Christians are born in the water of baptism through Jesus, who wishes all of us to be fishers of men.

Symbol of the
Four~Leaf Clover

The four-leaf clover is an age-old symbol of good fortune. The four leaves symbolize hope, faith, love and luck. Possessing a four-leaf clover is thought to charm the owner with protection, and the good luck is even greater if the clover is received as a gift. The mystique of the four-leaf clover lives on today since finding one is still a rare occurrence.

Symbol of the
Frog

Finding a frog brings good luck, and a wish made secretly upon seeing the first frog in spring will most certainly come true. Ancient cultures fashioned frog-shaped amulets to attract good luck, love and friends. Many cultures have relied on the frog as a weather forecaster. Frogs stay near water during rainy periods and will come out to wait for sunshine if the weather is going to improve.

Tradition of Garlic

Loved and loathed more than any other herb, garlic has been important to man for thousands of years. Essential in flavoring the cuisine of many cultures, garlic has been purported to ward off vampires and imbue soldiers with bravery and strength. To prevent disease, people hung garlic from their neck. A more proper place for this herb, however, is on your tree to inspire all with the lively flavor of the Christmas season.

Our Lady of Guadalupe

In 1531 near Mexico City, the Virgin Mary miraculously appeared before Juan Diego, an Aztec converted to Christianity. She urged him to have the city's bishops build a shrine, but they did not believe Diego. The Virgin reappeared with roses, impossible to grow in winter, as proof. He showed the bishops the roses wrapped in his cloak, which was miraculously imprinted with the image of the Virgin. Mexicans still pilgrimage to the Basilica of Guadalupe on December 12 in honor of Mexico's patron saint, the Lady of Guadalupe.

Guardian Angels

The dual role of guardian angels is to guide us to good thoughts and deeds, and to protect us from evil. The presence of guardian angels here on earth is taught in both the Old and New Testaments of the Bible. Psalm 91:11 reads, "For he shall give his angels charge of you, to guard you in all your ways." Guardian angels are portrayed as loving spirits who protect and guide us through life's many experiences.

Symbol of the Heart

For many centuries, the heart has been a symbol of love. Throughout pre-Christian and early Christian eras, it was believed to be the center of emotion. During the 16th century and the baroque period (1600-1750), the heart was recognized as a sign of sincerity and devotion. In many nations around the world today, the heart is the primary symbol of St. Valentine's Day, a holiday celebrating love.

Symbol of the
Hedgehog

A European symbol of rejuvenation and spring, the hedgehog is an adorable and inspiring creature. Native to the Eastern Hemisphere, these tiny animals are helpful in keeping harmful bugs under control. When frightened, the hedgehog turns into a prickly ball. When happy and safe, its coat feels soft, teaching us to be less defensive to better enjoy and appreciate life.

Legend of the
Holly

The bright red and green of holly make it a natural symbol of rebirth. Legends regarding this plant abound. According to one legend, holly branches bearing white berries were woven into Christ's crown of thorns. Since the blood of Christ stained the berries, they grow red on the holly branch to this day. Holly has also come to stand for peace and joy.

Symbol of the Hummingbird

The hummingbird symbolizes love, joy and beauty. Its unique ability to fly backward teaches us that we can look back at our past without dwelling there but continuing forward. The hummingbird's aptitude to hover while drinking nectar reminds us to savor each moment, appreciating its sweetness.

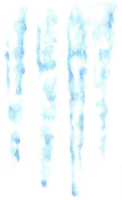

Legend of the Icicle

When Christ the Savior was born that first Christmas Eve, the heavenly angels cried in joyful adoration. Their tears of happiness gently fell to earth that crisp winter night, forming icicles on the edges of the stable and nearby evergreens. These tiny pendants of ice twinkled in the radiant starlight. To this day, icicle decorations are often used on Christmas trees as reminders of the joy celebrated over the birth of Christ the King.

Legend of the
Ladybug

According to European folklore, ladybugs symbolize good luck. Many years ago aphids invaded farmers' grapevines. When the farmers prayed for help to the Virgin Mary, legend tells us that swarms of little red beetles appeared. They proceeded to eat the aphids and save the crops. The farmers named the beetles ladybugs in honor of Mary, Our Lady.

Legend of the
Leprechaun
and his
Pot of Gold

Legend tells us the wee Irish folk called leprechauns make fairy shoes for a living. They are said to stash their gold in a pot at the end of the rainbow. The best way to find a leprechaun is to follow the tap of a shoemaker's hammer. If you catch him and can keep him in sight, he must take you to his treasure. If the leprechaun can trick you into looking away, he will vanish along with your hopes for finding his treasure.

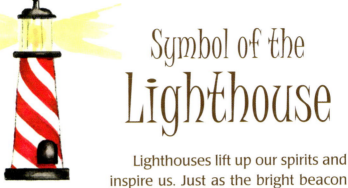

Symbol of the
Lighthouse

Lighthouses lift up our spirits and inspire us. Just as the bright beacon of light guides ships along their route, directing them away from danger, the lighthouse symbolizes guidance through life. The lighthouse also serves as a symbol of Christ, the light of the world. "Your word is a lamp to my feet and a light for my path." Psalm 119:105

Legend of the
Lily of the Valley

Legend claims that as the Virgin Mary cried at the crucifixion of Jesus, her tears fell softly and turned into a beautiful flower, the lily of the valley. Even today many people call these delicate, bell-shaped flowers Mary's tears. Lily of the valley is rich with the fragrance of springtime and new beginnings. These flowers also symbolize the sweetness, purity and rejuvenating qualities of Jesus Christ.

Symbol of
the
Lion

Majestic in stature, the lion is an emblem of power, strength, dignity and courage. The lion's yellow fur once symbolized the sun, and like most sun symbols, the lion came to represent Christ, the light of the world. Referred to as the king of the beasts, the lion continues as a symbol of might, justice, protection and conquest.

Symbol of the
Lion and the Lamb

The Bible tells us that when Jesus returns to Earth, all who were enemies will live together in harmony,  even the animals. The powerful lion will lie down with the gentle lamb, and love and peace will reign. Christian beliefs attribute the qualities of both the lion and the lamb to Jesus Christ, the Son of God. Embodied within Christ are the lion's majesty and might, as well as the lamb's innocence and gentleness. Love the complete Christ, both lion and lamb, and rejoice that he is King!

Symbol of the
Mistletoe

Long ago mistletoe symbolized divine love and healing. In Scandinavia mistletoe represented peace to enemies and lovers alike. When hung from the ceiling or in a doorway, it signifies harmony and goodwill. The current custom of kissing beneath the mistletoe is based on Scandinavian mythology.

Symbol of the
Mushroom

Associated with nature and the beauty of the forest, mushrooms are considered a good-luck symbol. Finding a mushroom is considered to be very lucky and mean good fortune is at hand. In Germany mushroom ornaments are displayed on Christmas trees in reverence for nature and in hope of good luck in the New Year.

Tradition of the Nutcracker

Nutcracker figurines originated in the Erzgebirge area of Germany as early as the 1700s. They were traditionally dressed as soldiers and kings. Villagers took satisfaction in having these authoritative figures perform the menial task of cracking nuts. Some may still crack nuts, but the real joy is their colorful presence decorating the home.

Symbol of the Owl

Throughout history owls have been credited with providing forewarning and good counsel. The owl's thoughtful and solemn appearance has generated its association with wisdom and virtue. Comparisons have been made between the owl's visual ability to pierce the darkness and the light of Christ dissolving the darkness of the world.

Tradition of the
Painted Egg

The Eastern European tradition of painting eggs developed as a result of their exchange as Easter presents. In many countries, eggs were a symbol of eternal life. The egg was likened to the tomb from which Christ arose. A desire to enhance the beauty of these Easter gifts led to the folk tradition of egg painting.

Legend of the
Panda

Long ago pandas were pure white. Chinese legend tells how the panda got its black and white coat. The ancient tale tells of a young girl who gave her life to save a snowy-white panda cub. The pandas were very sad and rubbed black ashes on their legs as a sign of mourning. They wiped their eyes, hugged each other and covered their ears with their paws. Wherever they touched themselves, the ashes stained their fur black.

Symbol of the
Peacock

Known as the bird with 100 eyes because of the iridescent, eye-like patterns in its beautiful tail, the peacock is a symbol of the all-seeing omniscience of God. Because it was believed that the flesh of the peacock never spoiled, it is also a symbol of immortality. After molting, a peacock's feathers are replaced by even more beautiful ones, illustrating the concept of resurrection.

Symbol of the
Peanut

The peanut is a symbol of the mystery and anticipation of the Christmas season. Just as a peanut's shell is opened to discover a hidden nut inside, the Christmas season unfolds with many wonderful surprises. In years past, family members often gathered to make handmade decorations, using peanuts and other gilded nuts to adorn the Christmas tree.

Tradition of the
Pickle Ornament

According to German tradition, the pickle brings good luck. After all the other ornaments were hung on the tree, the pickle ornament was hidden somewhere within the branches. On Christmas morning, the first child to find the gherkin was rewarded with an additional small present left by St. Nicholas. The pickle tradition encourages youngsters to enjoy the many ornaments on the tree before checking to see what St. Nick has brought them.

Symbol of the Pig

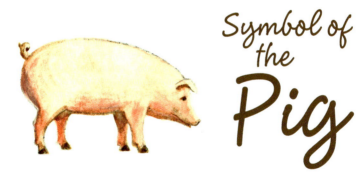

According to German tradition, partaking of a roast pork dinner on Christmas Eve will prevent evil and promote prosperity in the new year. Germans have a saying, "Wir haben Schwein," which means, "We have good luck." Pigs are considered to be symbols of good fortune, thrift and savings. Children are traditionally given piggy banks to encourage them to save.

Tradition of the
Piñata

The piñata may have originated in China and then spread to Italy, Spain and the Americas. Early piñatas were clay pots decorated with colored paper and filled with tiny treasures and treats. Used for religious teaching, its seven points represent the seven deadly sins. Breaking the piñata represents good defying evil. The treasures pouring from the broken piñata symbolize blessings, charity and abundance.

Tradition of the
Pineapple

The pineapple is a traditional American symbol of hospitality. When colonial sea captains returned from their tropical voyages, they would take pineapples from their cargo and hang them on their front door or gatepost as a sign of welcome and hospitality. Later, people began carving pineapple designs into doorways and gateposts. Pineapples are still given today as a symbol of welcome or friendship.

Tradition of the
Pine Cone

Because they withstand the cold of winter, evergreen trees are regarded as symbols of eternal life. Abundantly available, pine cones are widely used as natural decorations. Molds for pine cones were among the earliest developed by European glassblowers to reproduce the decoration as glass ornaments.

Legend of the
Poinsettia

Mexican legend tells of a boy who had no gift to put by the figure of the baby Jesus in church on Christmas Eve. On his way to church, he heard an angel tell him to pick some dried weeds for his gift. As he laid them beside the other gifts, the weeds turned into beautiful flowers. Dr. Joel Poinsett, the first U.S. ambassador to Mexico, brought the plant to the United States where it was named poinsettia.

Symbol of the
Polar Bear

Found in the Arctic north, the polar bear is considered by northern native peoples to be powerful, wise and almost human. Largest of the bear species, the polar bear survives in a harsh land where winter temperatures plummet for weeks at a time. The polar bear's success at hunting and trapping seals has led some to believe that polar bears are as intelligent as apes.

Tradition of the
Polish Star

In the Polish tradition of celebrating Christmas, the star has special significance. On Christmas Eve the first star of the night is named "Gwiazda," meaning "little star," in remembrance of the Star of Bethlehem. At the moment it appears, greetings and good wishes are exchanged. Families then partake of the Christmas supper, "Wigilia," the most carefully planned meal of the year.

Symbol of the
Pomegranate

Throughout the ages, the pomegranate, with its abundant seeds, has represented fertility, health and rebirth. A symbol of resurrection and everlasting life, the pomegranate is often pictured in Christian art with the Virgin Mary and infant Jesus. Parts of the plant have been used medicinally, and the pomegranate is featured in the coat of arms of several medical associations.

Tradition of the
Pretzel

Pretzels had their beginning in the 6th century at an Italian monastery. A young monk was preparing unleavened bread for Lent and creatively twisted scraps of bread dough to resemble arms folded in prayer. He named his creation "pretiola," a Latin word meaning "little reward," and gave it as a treat to children who recited their prayers. The pretzel is often served during Lent to remind Christians of their faith.

Symbol of the
Rainbow

Resembling a giant gate or bridge, the rainbow has been called by some the gateway to heaven. The Old Testament tells how God placed a rainbow in the sky following the Flood as a promise that he would never destroy the Earth by flood again. Therefore the rainbow has become a symbol of reconciliation between God and man.

Legend of the
Robin

The night that Christ was born a little brown bird shared the stable with the Holy Family. During the night, Joseph built a fire to keep the family warm, but as they slept, the fire burned out. The bird flew down from its nest and fanned the embers with its wings, drawing so close to the fire that the heat turned the bird's feathers red. The breast of the robin has been red ever since to remind us of its love and compassion for the baby Jesus.

Legend of the
Rooster

Legend states that the only time the rooster crowed at midnight was the night that Jesus was born. In Spanish and Latin American countries, "Misa del Gallo," the Mass of the Rooster, is celebrated at midnight on Christmas Eve. The crowing of the rooster at the dawn of each morning symbolizes the daily triumph of light over darkness and the victory of good over evil.

St. Anthony

Christians believe St. Anthony, a faithful servant of Christ, is able to find all things lost or stolen. According to legend, this attribute can be traced back to an incident in St. Anthony's life. When his cherished book of Psalms was stolen, St. Anthony prayed to God that it would be found. The thief was so moved by St. Anthony's faith that he returned the book. To this day, people pray through St. Anthony to find lost and stolen articles.

St. Christopher

According to legend, St. Christopher asked a hermit how he could serve Christ. The hermit suggested that St. Christopher use his tremendous size and strength to assist people across a dangerous river. One day a small child asked to be carried across the rushing water. St. Christopher had never felt anything so heavy. The child pronounced, "You had on your shoulders not only the whole world, but also he who made it. I am Christ your king." To this day, St. Christopher is lovingly known as the patron saint of travelers for his assistance with safe passage.

St. Francis of Assisi

St. Francis of Assisi, born in 1182, is the Catholic patron saint of animals and the environment. Legend tells us that St. Francis could communicate with animals. He is credited with popularizing use of the Nativity scene to share the hope and joy of God's love. The son of a wealthy cloth merchant, St. Francis converted from a worldly youth to a poor, humble religious life of caring for the sick, especially lepers. St. Francis founded the Franciscan Order in 1209.

St. Nicholas... Santa Claus

The concept of the American Santa Claus originated with St. Nicholas, who was born in Asia Minor about 280. He was known as a kind, benevolent man and made a saint because of his generosity. In honor of St. Nicholas, December 6 became the traditional day in Europe for the exchange of Christmas gifts and the beginning of the holiday season. Dutch immigrants to the United States brought with them their version of the gift-giving St. Nicholas, known as "Sinter Klass." Americans, unaccustomed to the Dutch pronunciation, turned this into "Santa Claus," who is beloved as a symbol of Christmas by children of all ages.

St. Patrick

Born around 385 in Scotland, St. Patrick is credited with bringing Christianity to Ireland. At age 14, Irish raiders seized Patrick to be a slave. He later escaped and reunited with his family. A dream called him back to Ireland where, until his death on March 17, 461, Patrick preached the Gospel and built churches throughout the country. A very important holiday to the Irish, St. Patrick's Day is a traditional time for spiritual renewal.

Symbol of the Sand Dollar

The markings on the shell of the sand dollar symbolize the birth, crucifixion and resurrection of Christ. The bottom of the sand dollar bears the outlines of a Christmas poinsettia and bell. On the top side of the shell, a five-pointed star representing the Star of Bethlehem is surrounded by the outline of an Easter lily. The five narrow openings in the shell symbolize the four nail holes and spear wound made in the body of Christ during the crucifixion. When a shell is broken, five doves of peace are found inside, signifying the goodwill and peace sung by the angels the first Christmas morning.

Santa's Magic Key

Dear Santa, we have no chimney as you can plainly see, and I was terribly worried that you'd pass over me. We hung this very special key outside, right by the door. Then Mom told me to jump in bed, not to worry anymore. Your magic will make this key fit, to open up our door, so you can come inside tonight and tip-toe 'cross the floor.

Symbol of the
Shamrock

The shamrock, one of the most widely recognized symbols of Ireland, has been considered good luck since the earliest of times. Legend says St. Patrick used the shamrock to teach pagans the doctrine of the Holy Trinity. Just as three leaves make up one shamrock, three persons (Father, Son and Holy Spirit) are in one God.

Tradition of the
Snowman

For centuries children have gleefully awaited the winter's first snowfall. Rolling large balls of that fluffy gift from heaven, they delight in making their own special companion. Completed with a carrot for a nose, coal for the eyes and mouth, and sticks for arms, the snowman truly does come to life for the children who created their frosty friend.

symbol of the
STAR

The star symbolizes that great light which led the wise men to the Christ child so many years ago. Throughout much of the world today, the Christian holiday begins with the appearance of the first star on Christmas Eve. The star also symbolizes the hope for peace and good fortune, and demonstrates the fact that people, regardless of their nationality, share the same universe.

Symbol of the
Star of
Bethlehem

Because of its prominence in the Nativity story, the Star of Bethlehem is one of the most powerful symbols of Christianity. On Christmas Eve, the Star, shining brightly in the heavens, guided the wise men to the lowly manger where the Christ child was born. Matthew 2:2 reads, "For we have seen his star in the East and have come to worship him."

Symbol of the
Starfish

According to legend, starfish are reflections of stars in the sky inhabiting the ocean floor. Symbolizing rebirth, starfish have a remarkable ability for regeneration. If a starfish is cut in half, two starfish will grow. The limbs of the starfish work together for the benefit of the whole, illustrating equality and teamwork.

Symbol of the
Stork

According to European folklore, the idea of storks delivering babies to waiting parents sprung from the belief that storks nesting and raising their own young upon roofs and chimneys was a sign of good fortune and blessing. Households placed sweets on their windowsill, letting the stork know their wish for a sweet infant of their own. When parents needed to explain to their little ones how babies arrived, the stork was a welcome answer. Even today these gentle birds are considered a symbol of abundant good fortune.

Symbol of the Sunflower

At one time, the sunflower was considered to be a symbol of adoration, possibly because it follows the path of the sun as it travels across the sky. The yellow petals of the sunflower imitate the sun's rays, and the heart-shaped leaves on the strong stalk help to absorb the sun's light. The sunflower is the perfect example for us to follow the Son of Man and to grow in his love and presence.

Legend of the Tabby Cat

Legend tells us that as the baby Jesus shivered in the manger on the night he was born, a tiny kitten jumped into the humble crib to warm him with its fur. Mary touched the little tabby cat to thank it for its gifts of love and warmth, bestowing her initial "M" on its forehead. Since that day, tabby cats have been known for the characteristic "M" on their foreheads, a symbol of gratitude for love so gently given.

Symbol of the Teapot

The brewing of tea in a pot dates back nearly 5,000 years to ancient China.

In many parts of the world, brewing and serving tea involves great ceremony.

The teapot itself has become a symbol of hospitality in the home.

Symbol of the Turtle

Taking their homes with them wherever they go, turtles remind us to remember our roots while still welcoming new places and phases in life. They teach us to appreciate life's simple, true necessities: shelter, food, drink and most importantly, faith. The turtle's slow gait requires the animal to have faith that it will eventually get where it is going and that its needs will be satisfied along the way.

Legend of the Unicorn

The mythical unicorn has long been a source of enchantment. Solitary, swift and graceful, the unicorn had a single spiraling horn growing from its forehead. Sought by many, the unicorn's horn was said to have medicinal and magical properties. According to legend, the unicorn disregarded Noah's call to board the ark, preferring to frolic in the rains of the Flood. Ever since, unicorns exist only in our imaginations.

Tradition of Wine

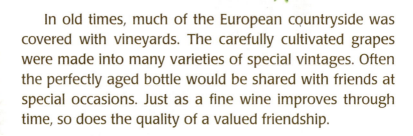

In old times, much of the European countryside was covered with vineyards. The carefully cultivated grapes were made into many varieties of special vintages. Often the perfectly aged bottle would be shared with friends at special occasions. Just as a fine wine improves through time, so does the quality of a valued friendship.

Symbol of the
Wreath

The Christmas wreath has decorated many a door with fresh greenery. Wreaths are often made of evergreens, including holly, mistletoe, pine and fir. Because they are green and bear fruit in the winter when other plants appear lifeless and bare, evergreens signify God's immortality and everlasting life. The wreath's circular shape reminds us of the circles of life, family and love.

Tradition of the
Yule Log

An ancient tradition originating in Europe, the yule log warmed the house during the cold Christmas night. It was ceremoniously brought to the fireplace and lit with the remnants of the log from the previous year. This was to erase trouble from the past and bring good fortune and protection from fire. Today the yule log takes the form of a traditional French cake shaped like a log, a perfect finish to a Christmas feast.